GW01066365

Jan 2009
For Harold
with thanks
Joanne

Abel Books

Published by Abel Publishing

info@abelpublishing.com
www.abelpublishing.com

First published on 25 November 2008
by Abel Publishing

A CIP catalogue record for this book
is available from the British Library

Printed and bound in Great Britain by
Stanley L. Hunt (Printers) Ltd
Midland Road, Rushden, Northants

ISBN: 978-0-9559423-1-0

Thank you to all those who have helped
to make this book possible
especially my parents

On a poet's lips I slept
Dreaming like a love-adept
In the sound his breathing kept;
Nor seeks nor finds he mortal blisses,
But feeds on the aërial kisses
Of shapes that haunt thought's wildernesses.
He will watch from dawn to gloom
The lake-reflected sun illume
The yellow bees in the ivy-bloom,
Nor heed nor see, what things they be;
But from these create he can
Forms more real than living man,
Nurselings of immortality!
One of these awaken'd me,
And I sped to succour thee.

(from 'Prometheus Unbound', Fourth Spirit,
Percy Bysshe Shelley)

An Italian Connection
(Autumn 2008)

An Autumn Suffering

Dozing under an autumn sun
Chin resting on chest, scorched flesh on flesh
Lids limply closed, arms taut
Fully stretched, across the cliff face, wet
Wet from the scrotum-tightening water
Now just gently heaving and swelling
Below the Roman bridge, not far from Gova

Dozing under an autumn sun
He sleeps the sleep of millennia
His pain and tormentor
Perhaps at last receded?
He rests, and only now and then
Opens his eyes, raises his head
And surveys the great panorama
To which he's endlessly bound

Dozing under an autumn sun
The comforting Madonna at his feet
He gradually perceives gambolling gazelles
Hears the jays' cacophonous calling
The green woodpeckers' laughter
As he listens for the grasshoppers' chirps
Tastes on his chapped lips the honeyed air
And finally inhales the promising harvest

And dozing under an autumn sun
The torture lessened, to the moment yielding
He suddenly yells a primeval scream
A cry of centuries; of suffering insurmountable
Which ricochets throughout the valleys
Drowns the hunters' guns, the dogs' howling
Eclipses the full moon and searing sun's rays
Until it fells the circling eagle: his heart's prey

Costa di Morsiano, Villa Minozza, Italy, 19 Oct 2008

Abandoned to the Hawks

Abandoned to the crows, wild boar, stalking hawks
This humble dwelling looks more like a hovel
Than an abode which sheltered life, nurtured seed

Cracked and crumbled, its shape now a mystery
Its destiny an illusion, it rests on the hill
Quite oblivious to time, to its defining story

This ruin on the hill's shored up by thrusting trees
By unruly roots and branches, once maintained, pruned
That now spread in abandonment to the caprice of moods

Veiled in bluish autumn mist, the ruin still glows:
Cloak of leaves all ablaze; stoked by the sun's last ebbing rays
Though its folk, its dwellers, have long since departed

And with them the oxen, lambs and trusty old donkey
And far-travelled camels: these creatures of witness
Harbingers of faith have long since dissolved, like the myth

Yet with this ruin, with this one-time sacred sanctuary
Passing seasons, life, ageing, death once contained meaning
Were commemorated with an ultimate and eternal unity of being

Costa di Morsiano, Villa Minozza, Italy, 12 Oct 2008

Man with the Barrow

And in his calm gaze
Slightly drawn to his feet
He carries
The lost centuries,
And on his lean head
A faded straw hat
Of decades long passed
Sits perched,
As before him he pushes
His rusty old barrow

Clothed in dark smocks
So measurably he strolls
Clocking curves
Of life
Suspended on the mount,
As far above the tree-line
He emerges so surely
Averting deep crevasses
With deft motions
Of his wrists

Is he emptying or
Filling it?
Nobody knows,

But what's in it
His load
From morning to dusk
Seems essential
Though not heavy
As he wheels it
Smoothly and leisurely
As if carrying
Free time

Costa di Morsiano, Villa Minozza, Italy, 9 Oct 2008

The Poet and The Madman
(For Saadi Yousef)

Around us a motley gathering of men
Roughly dressed, of differing ages
Supping their wine
Coffee, grappa,
And though each at his own table
They throw odd remarks
To one another,
While the mad man
Not locked away
And still part of the village
Interjects with words
Hard to decipher
And greets passers-by
Always by first name
Cheerily, loudly
Though they seldom reply

Then I turn to the poet
Alone in contemplation
Head bowed, hands on knees
Eyes wide open
Finger-tips lightly touching
Thumbs turned upwards
As he rotates them
Gently from his body
Then towards it
His head finally nodding

Slowly, pensively
As if finding accord
With his murmuring reflections
With his intimate musings
His mind and body
Now attuned as one

Costa di Morsiano, Villa Minozza, Italy, 7 Oct 2008

Donna Fatale of the Bar

'When the apples fall
The leaves will follow'
Whispers Donna Fatale
Leaning languorously
Towards me;
Her bare autumn fruit
Now slightly wizen
Loosely dangling
Awaiting one last shake
Before acceding to the Fall

'And tonight it may yet happen'
She prophesizes like a siren
Overfilling my wine
Just a little
So the liquid trickles
Slowly down the sides
Wetting her svelte fingers
Before she gives me
Its dark content
And a smile that lingers
Knowingly
Wantonly

'And when the leaves follow...'
She murmurs softly
To the night
Before brushing

Her damp fingers
Deftly round my lobes
Fondling hairs and skin
Which naturally respond
Though my will
Is to resist

'Ah, the apples are so ripe
Yearning for the Fall...'
She teasingly remarks
Then abruptly withdraws
As finally I succumb
Eclipse my mind's
Stark warnings
And lurch
For those loose breasts
Search for
Half-hid nipples
Yet only grasp
Dank air

Costa di Morsiano, Villa Minozza, Italy, 9 Oct 2008

* Written from the male perspective and fantasy.

Rosa in Montefiorino

And as I awake
I rise in a land
Of rose-flushed jays
Flowing red wine
Undulating fells
Russet-hued scarps
Gambolling gazelles

And as I awake
Blushed by Aurora
I rise from the Rocca:
Refuge of the free
Of martyred souls
Bloody battles won
Bastion of liberty

And as I awake
Perfumed by flowers
Cushioned by meadows
I reach for the sun
Now rising in the East
And leave the dry 'Dragon'
Strewn around my feet

And as I awake
To this primal morn
Chimed by poplar trees
Singing cicadas
Heart-shaped leaves
I embrace the first dew
And gently stride forth

Costa di Morsiano, Villa Minozza, Italy, 3 Oct 2008

* *Rosa is an allusion to Rosa Luxemburg who stood for social justice and freedom of thought and actions. She was brutally murdered, then her body was thrown into a canal and was not found for many months. The Rocca at Montefiorino was where the first Communist Republic was declared in 1944. 'La Dragone' is the name of the river below. This poem is a sequel to 'Freedom of Mind in Rosa', composed in 2004.*

Bones of War
(A Poem for Peace)

Bones of War

From out of the mire
The swamp
And the bog
Hideously
Stealthily
It reared
Its gruesome head –
Fleshed out
Warm-blooded
And expectant
It snatched you –
You roared
A silent roar
A roar unheard
Full of dread

The skeleton of war
Needed arming
Needed padding
Cried out
To be fed

No matter
Whence you came
To where
You might have fled
No matter
What colour
What creed,
Your country –
That elusive state –

Bones of War

Needed
YOU!
Requisitioned
You,
As its own
Flesh and blood

The skeleton of war
Needed arming
Needed padding
Cried out
To be fed

Countless tons
Of blood
A million
Pounds of flesh
Could not suffice
Would not
Satiate
Its appetite
Its needy hate,
As it thrust

Forwards
Sideways
Backwards,
Flailing
As it pleased

The skeleton of war
Needed arming
Needed padding
Cried out
To be fed

Joanne Maria McNally

'More flesh!
More flesh!'
Was its rallying cry:
'No matter
What country
No matter
What creed!
Bring out your son
Your grandson
Your daughter
Your niece!'
The skeleton
Knew no division
For the quenching
Of its needs

The skeleton of war
Needed arming
Needed padding
Cried out
To be fed

The skeleton of war –
First falteringly
Now steadily
Now
With some haste
Soon gained
In momentum
Stirred by lust
By a strengthened
More purposeful
Gait –

Bones of War

Was fed
From the left
From the right
Of the lands
From the poor
From the gentry
So great
Were its demands.
It continued its march
Across continents
And by sea,
Trampling
This way and that
With no one to heed,
Swallowing
Most in its path
Scourging
Landscapes at will,
Still siphoning
More blood
In order to fill
Its own
Ghastly wounds
And ever-
Shedding
Flesh

The skeleton of war
Needed arming
Needed padding
Cried out
To be fed

Joanne Maria McNally

Bones of War

'We must stop it!'
Was the plea
Now deployed
From all sides;
All exhausted
Depleted
Ravaged
And in need
Of advice:
'The Achilles heel
Must be found
Before
We're all doomed
With no land
Left to fight for
No folk left
To conquer
No resources
To exhume,
For the skeleton's
As hungry as ever!'
The generals
Politicians
And industrialists
Conclude

This pause for breath
New sense
And a touch
Of common good

Joanne Maria McNally

Bones of War

Surprisingly
Fortuitously
Seemed enough
To halt and hinder
The skeleton
Of death
Destruction
And belligerent deeds,
As it began
To crum *b le*
Implode
Chronically
Crr r ack
And tear   apart
At the seams

The skeleton of war
Lack ing arming

Lacking padd ing
SCREAMED out
To be fed

With its stride
Now curtailed
And its life-line
Suppressed
Its face
Now
Disintegrated
No longer
Expressed

Joanne Maria McNally

Bones of War

The horrors
Of its nature
The terrors
Of its regime
As it sank
Below the earth
Devouring
Spent generations
Ne'er again
To be seen

The skeleton of war
No longer

Armed

No longer

Padded

Duly buried

Its ugly

Head

Joanne Maria McNally

'May it be buried
For all time!'
Was the cry
From all sides
'Let's make peace,
No longer war!'
Was the unified
Rallying call,
'Let's embrace
One another,
Let's be happy
As one:
At one
With our earth
And no more
An ally to war!'

Hove, 23 September 2004

Knowing
(A Poem about the Past)

You knew me as a child.
And before me, you knew my mum.
You and Mon, your girlfriend, would baby-sit for mum. Mum was bridesmaid at yours and Mon's wedding. That was June 1945.
Later I would come to your house.
The house in which you still live. The house in which you have spent over half a century.
Your house was also my home.
Now and again we'd have a sing-along. Your daughter would take out her guitar, which you'd taught her how to play.
You'd also play the harmonica.
You'd played for fellow inmates many years before when you were a prisoner of war in Poland.
Your daughter taught me the basic chords and the folk song 'Home, home on the range, where the deer and the antelope play...' That song must have sounded different to you. As a seven-year old, home was something you took for granted.
It was just there, it was where you belonged and it would always be there.
I didn't know.
When we left the village, we lost touch. Mon died in her prime, and you mourned her loss daily. Nana would see you pass her house on your way to Mon's grave. You visited her every day.
You still visit.
You and mum never lost touch. If you were ever in town, you'd often pop in on mum. I'd see you at Christmas, when you dropped by with a card and

sometimes stayed for a drink. That was in my
college days when I was studying German.
And all those years you were communicating in
German.
I never knew.
You never said.
And now our paths have converged again.
My work on Germany's past has led me back to
you. And I have found you right in the middle of
Europe's darkest chapter. You'd been part of it.
You'd lived through it.
I never knew.
You never said.
We were told that you had worked on a farm in
Poland during the war and had been treated well.
We were happy with this.
At Christmas you gave me tapes you'd made over
thirty years ago.
You say so much.
And now we speak about those times.
I wonder about destiny.
You were a prisoner, a 'peat-bog soldier', you wore
clogs, you dug ditches, you sang songs.
You experienced hardship and brutality.
But also comradeship and solidarity.
You are one of the millions I've just written about.
I didn't know.
You didn't know.
Now we know.
You were marched for days on end first north-
eastwards in 1940, then westwards in 1945.

You were on a death march.
You never knew.
At Christmas I finished my work on the 'peat-bog soldiers' – the first victims of the German camp system – and then you gave me the tapes.
I listened and then I knew.
I suddenly knew why I had written what I had.
I sensed it came from somewhere deep within.
Until then, it had been a journey, the purpose of which was a mystery to me. I had been in spirit, where you had been half a century before.
I didn't know.
I had followed the journey of millions, and, at the end of it, I encountered yours.
I encountered your suffering, your steadfastness, your kindness, your unbroken spirit and humour, in spite of it all.
You had come through the hell of Sosnowitz, part of the Auschwitz complex, and had survived the evacuation march.
Many were less lucky.
We never knew.
At about the same time I also finished my work on Theresienstadt, a ghetto-cum-concentration camp for Jews.
Here, too, paths crossed.
Dr Rossel, chief inspector of the International Red Cross, provides the link. He was inspecting the conditions in the camps. He visited the Jews in Theresienstadt, North of Prague.
That was June 1944.

Soon afterwards he also visited you in your camp
in Teschen.
You never knew.
He then tried to visit you in Sosnowitz on 19
January 1945.
You were already on the move, along with the
inmates of Auschwitz. 14 000 British prisoners
from that same area were also on the move some
days later.
Sandwiched between the Red Army from the East
and the Allies from the West, marching in chaos,
were also countless different groups of people:
Russian prisoners of war, political prisoners, Jews,
gypsies, gays and refugees.
Some hard on your heels; some only a road apart.
Millions of people.
You didn't know.
Your column was on the back roads.
Three thousand of you when you set off.
You were marched through the spoils of war and
racial hatred. You witnessed the corpses, the
crimson snow. You stumbled over bodies.
For one desolate moment you saw the others.
Without shirts, shoes, souls.
Empty of spirit, painfully brittle, the last breath of
being whipped out of them.
Why, what for?
We still don't know.
That was near the border to Czechoslovakia.

You were not much better off yourselves. Yet you all
hissed as one of the Jews was killed with one kick,
because he could no longer stand.
When you booed, they stopped. Then the column
continued its march in the opposite direction.
Shrouded in ghostly silence.
One Jew less.
You were on your way to Stalag 344, then onto
Nürnberg. Nürnberg was still hundreds of miles
and many weeks of marching away.
You never knew.
They never said.
And yet they knew.
Your journey was destined to end in Nürnberg.
My journey began there over half my life-time ago.
That was when I began writing letters in German.
You had begun your correspondence in German in
1946.
Over all those years you've kept in touch with
Marie, the daughter of the farmer in Poland.
Your friendship across cultures has outstretched the
Cold War.
We never knew.
You never said.
Your friendship is more important than any peace
agreement.
It's from the heart.
It's not manufactured, nor staged.
It just is.
And that genuine warmth has outlived the
makeshift animosity between nations.

It has been passed onto the next generations.
We know.
You were both young when you last saw each other almost sixty years ago. Marie was barely a teenager and you were in your early twenties. You had a whole future ahead of you; and you were both present in each other's.
It was a warm presence, not an intrusive one.
Marie's first son was born on your birthday.
She knew it was your birthday, yet you did not know hers.
Your birthday had been celebrated at their farm all those years ago. By so-called enemies. In the midst of war. You shared their company and their food. They took photos of you. They sent these to your family. They treated you well.
They trusted you completely.
These acts of human kindness undermined the National Socialists' ideology. The Nazis did not want the enemy to get so close.
The people of this area had to work within the new political and racial structures.
They did not always accept the Nazi terms.
That we know.
You became one of the family.
That we knew.
Marie's family's farm had been a brief refuge for you during the hardship. You also helped them. Their three horses, four cows and a few pigs and chickens became your own.
You'd been a farmer before being called up.

Your father had a farm. As a farmer you should never have been called up. Your mates were in the home guard; you were part of the reinforcements for the 2nd Battalion Lincolnshire regiment. They were in Belgium.
Your father tried to get you discharged.
He wrote to the Foreign Office. The Foreign Office realised their mistake. When a telegram for your release was issued, you were already on the ship to France.
You never knew.
They never said.
It was too late. The eight weeks' training for fighting became a five-year 'tour' of Europe.
'A real Cook's tour of Europe courtesy of the Führer,' you said.
The Führer was brutally indifferent to yours and others' suffering – the life of a single German is worth more than the lives of twenty Britishers, he once said.
He never visited a prisoner of war camp; he never visited a concentration or extermination camp.
He never knew.
Marie's father's farm was in the heart of the Polish Corridor, the 'Reichsgau Wartheland'. They'd worked their fifteen acres for years. They'd seen the comings and goings of different peoples, the toings and froings of pieces of land.
The taking over of property.

They'd seen the hundreds of thousands of 'ethnic' Germans from central Europe flood into the area.
The Führer had invited them.
That was 1942 at the height of 'Germanisation'.
At the end of the war these settlers became refugees.
At about the same time the family's farm was taken over by Poles from the East. The region reverted back to its Polish names.
The German language and the German names were mostly wiped from memory.
But you still knew.
For a few years after the war, Marie and her family became like you – slave labourers working for others and scattered around the province, separated from family and friends. Her father, a member of the Home Guard during the war, ended up in the camp where you had also been interned some years before.
He was labelled a collaborator.
Marie worked in Schildberg near Breslau for a while.
Another place where you'd also been a prisoner.
It felt strange when you knew.
Working detachments became your life for many of your exile years. You were often better off than in the base camps, where boredom and madness soon took hold. There, many prisoners went 'camp happy'. They took imaginary dogs for walks, played games with fleas, and turned maybugs into flying propellers.
In the early days they also died like flies.

Victims of dysentery.
You said.
You did not shy away from the heavy work.
You couldn't. You learned to dig canals, build roads, dredge ditches. It was the only time in your life you ever had a suntan. Two months in the Riviera could not have browned you as well.
Having not shaven for months, and dressed in any old uniform, you looked more like castaways than soldiers.
We never knew.
There was no sign of habitation where you worked. The bleak desolation was only broken now and again by sandy covered hills, and the stacks of peat.
Without a mucker you would not have survived long.
You knew.
It was on your first working party at Konin, when you were digging the peat, that you met your mate. The bond was instant.
You could talk about home together.
His home was ten miles from yours. You shared the same contours, the same dialect. You talked about your girlfriends back home. By the end of the war you knew each other's sweethearts as if they were your own. Throughout the years of captivity you became inseparable.
You shared everything, you made the same choices. You ended up in the same places.

When Fred's feet became like lumps of raw meat on the death march, you did all the foraging for food in the evenings. He could rest.
When he grew weary with pain from the endless marching, you chivvied him along.
Your friendship and solidarity would last a life-time. Marie still talks about Fred.
You still phone his wife.
You remember.
By mid 1941 the make-shift camps had been turned into proper prisoner of war camps.
Red Cross parcels began to arrive; uniforms and boots were issued. You had cigarettes and enough food. You longed, though, for different company.
Letters to loved ones back home could now be sent.
You were alive.
They finally knew.
The working parties continued.
Still wearing clogs you broke up gravestones on your next detachment. That was near Posen.
The gravestones were Jewish.
You'd sit with a hammer beside the road breaking up the symbols of past lives. You packed the pieces into the bottom of the road.
You watched them disappear beneath the layers.
You thought about their lives.
What they knew.
The Jewish graveyard was at one end of the compound. Often the German corporal in charge would run round it firing his revolver in the air.
Why?

You didn't know.
You tell many comical tales. The tricks you used to get up to on the farms.
You tell of Snooks, the young Londoner, thrown as though in a high wind from the horse that bolted.
Or 'Swanny', the newspaper correspondent, who was dragged down the road for miles by his cows as they galloped away with him. He was too proud to let go. Then there was Jim who used to get his cows mixed up and put them in the wrong stalls. And 'Yorkie' from Leeds, who nearly lost the mayor's Christmas dinner to a dog. He was carrying it down the high street to the baker to be cooked when the dog snatched it from the basket and ran off with it. 'Yorkie' got it back – a bit second-hand, though.
The farms were a cushy number.
When you had to leave the farms, the people were sorry to see you go.
They'd accepted you.
They liked you.
You had different kinds of guards at your next place. The Germans were scraping the barrel by this time, you said. They'd either passed the sell-by date, or were strange in more ways than one.
That was 1943. In this place you dug trenches. You looked after the horses coming back from the Russian front. You played football.
The footballing cost you many bribes.
On New Year's Eve, Percy Foreman, 'the mad professor', blew up a landmine at midnight. He'd

been preparing it for months. Gathering up bits of scrap metal. He wanted to surprise the lads.
What became your treat, was the guards' greatest fear. They thought the Russians had arrived. When they heard the blast, they darted off in all directions. The worse for drink.
It was like stirring up a hornets' nest, you said.
Humour holds your account together; humour is what held you together. In spite of it all.
Yet, as a corporal (your promotion in June 1940 was postponed due to the surrender) you would have been exempt from work.
Under the Geneva Convention.
But the Geneva Convention counted for little under the Führer's regime.
That you knew.
We didn't.
Your final detachment, a mine at Sosnowitz, is devoid of humour. It was in the industrial belt of Poland, breath-takingly close to Auschwitz.
You worked for the SS.
We never knew,
you never knew,
and yet they knew.
The civilian authorities were looking for workers.
The overcrowding of stalag VIIIB, Teschen, had become intolerable. You were all desperate to escape.
Oblivious to your fate, you joined a new working party.
The area was Auschwitz.
You only now know.

There were some fifty or more working parties from your camp in the area. 11 000 or so Commonwealth prisoners. When you agreed to go, the Red Army was less than a hundred and fifty miles away.
You didn't know.
They knew.
You should never have had to go to the area.
You were being sent to a war-zone.
It was against the Geneva Convention.
Relatives at home became more anxious with every mile of the Russians' advance. Stalin was heading straight for your area.
For his 'gold'.
He wanted the factories and mines intact.
Your work was his loot.
You didn't know.
The conditions in your work-place were some of the worst. You hacked and shovelled coal. You waded waist-high through streams of water, twelve hours on end, seven days a week.
You heard the blasts of the exploding seams.
You didn't know what was happening. You didn't have light in your lamps. The supplies of lighters and matches were not distributed to you for fear of sabotage.
Safety regulations were disregarded; fans regularly broke down. Accidents were routine.
Death was common.
You got sick.
For a farmer used to the open-air this must have been sheer purgatory.

Many Maoris had been there for years.
They knew.
Self-mutilation became their way of escaping the death trap. Evading the brutality of certain overseers.
You got pleurisy.
The German doctor allowed you a few days in bed.
If he had sent you straight back down the mine, you would have died.
He knew.
Very rarely did you have a day off.
The German civilian authorities wanted to increase your output to the maximum.
The military authorities knew, but they had little say.
Representations were made to the German High Command and Foreign Office in Berlin. Berlin passed the matter to the Ministry of Labour. The Ministry of Labour had little to say.
As the bureaucratic battles went round and round in circles, your labour was exploited to the extreme.
Your labour was fuelling IG Farben. IG Farben was supplying the gas chambers. The gas chambers were exterminating the Jews, the gypsies and many other Europeans.
You didn't know.
By the time you arrived at Sosnowitz, autumn 1944, the killing machines at Auschwitz had almost ground to a halt. We had yet to hear about Auschwitz. You didn't see the thick black smoke; you didn't smell the burning flesh.

You didn't know.
Other unlucky British prisoners of war knew more.
They became corpse-stokers.
We didn't know.
They didn't say.
The horror was too great.
The ovens' frenzied operation during the summer months had already done their worst. They'd just about 'destroyed the evidence'.
The millions of pounds of smoke had dispersed.
The souls, though, remained.
We know.
Then you became a 'foot-slogger'.
Force-marched halfway across Europe, without transport. The US had refused to provide motor trucks for the evacuation of prisoners.
They said it was the duty of the Germans to supply them. The Germans had none to spare. Or just didn't care. As the two powers quibbled for months about duties, you fought for survival.
You fought the hardest battle of your life. With no 'disposal instructions' issued and with the Red Army at the doorstep, you were hurriedly evacuated from Sosnowitz.
Your clothing and boot situation were no match for the snow blizzards and sub-zero temperatures.
You were told to travel light.
Why did the Nazis move you all so suddenly?
Why was there so much panic?
We will never know.
The documents disappeared.

The inmates from Auschwitz main camp were just behind you. You were ordered to march westwards to Stalag 344.
Stalag 344 was emptied of prisoners to make room for you. They were destined for Stalag VIIIA in Goerlitz.
Before you got there, you were ordered to march in another direction. Goerlitz was already full.
All the time squeezed either side by the advancing armies, and out of reach for the relief supplies.
Occasionally you were marched through the night.
It was a race against time.
For you it was another hell.
Who was co-ordinating this chaos?
What was the purpose?
Who knew?
The military authorities observed the patterns of the marches from above. Once they found you (it took them some weeks), they kept a track on the movements, they recorded the directions, they found out where you were from.
With no proper collapse officially acknowledged, with no responsibility for civilians and prisoners of war formally accepted, with no proper back-up arrangements in place for evacuation, supplies and maintenance, they became complicit and confused bystanders.
They knew.
We didn't.
They were helpless.

Millions of you became trapped in the fighting zones.
As the powers of the Gestapo and SS increased, the military advancements took priority over the movement of others.
The more Germany was squeezed, the worse your situation became.
Himmler was not interested in prisoners of war.
You were also part of the evidence he wanted to destroy.
Foraging for food, and ending up boiling grass or some fodder when the day's marching was over, sleeping in barns, at times in fields at night, watchful of the guards and their nervousness by day, dragging your feet along in a state of semi-consciousness, soaked through to the bone, you were still unbeaten.
They knew.
Your column moved along in a series of painful jerks.
You were dodging the Russians, toing and froing into Sudetenland.
You covered nearly nine hundred miles over roundabout routes by the end of the 'tour'.
At Luck, the Red Cross convoy finally caught up with you.
With food in your bellies your steps became lighter.
You still had hundreds of miles to cover.
You didn't know.
Czech civilians risked their lives to ease your suffering. They placed food in the ditches for you.

They offered you parcels as you passed through.
You were grateful for this. The Germans were not.
You saw one of your men killed at point blank
range. He'd stepped out to take a parcel.
He was buried on the spot.
His hunger extinguished.
With the smell and sound of spring in the air as
you marched along the Danube, your spirits lifted,
the going was good.
You appreciated the clear blue skies and the warmth
of the sun, the beautiful scenery and the little
castles perched on high.
German troops passing you day and night were
less heartened. They were indifferent to the weather
and their surroundings.
Their condition was dire.
They knew they were beaten.
You knew they were beaten.
You felt pity.
In spite of it all.
At Landshut in Southern Germany you became a
free man. Freed by General 'Blood and Guts'
Patton's 3rd American Army. A couple of weeks
later you had your first flight.
You were on your way home.
That was 12 May 1945.
You and Fred got as far as Lincoln by public
transport. Then you had to hitch. Hitching was
difficult because petrol was rationed. Rationing
meant restrictions on distances.

A driver stopped to take you five miles nearer home.
When he heard how long you'd been away, he broke
the rules and took you right to the door.
To the door of Ben's Farm..
Home.
You never saw him again.
When you arrived in the village the church bells
were ringing.
They were welcoming you home.
The whole village had turned up.
They knew.
They'd heard about your telegraph just hours before.
Your family was waiting; Mon was waiting.
You were confused.
They didn't know.
The next month was the happiest of your life.
You and Mon spent every waking minute together
walking in the fields, chatting and joking.
You became a VIP for a month – going from one
invitation to the next.
Although you talked a lot, they still didn't know.
You couldn't really say.
We would never really know.
On your wedding day, 14 June 1945, the whole
village turned out again. It was the beginning of
your new life.
When Mon died, you made the tapes.
We've listened to the tapes.
Now we think we know.

* This reflective poem (November 2002) was my spontaneous response to my relative's oral account and to my own original research findings about this bleak period of history: that is to say my response to 'difficult knowledge' (Hugh MacDiarmid).
The short poem 'Crossroads of Hell' (towards the end of this collection) preceded it.
This is a tribute to former soldier-prisoners of war forced to work in this area and who suffered immeasurably at the time, and who have suffered great injustices since in terms of lack of recognition of their hardship and ongoing failures to compensate them or to pass on withheld military payments.
Furthermore, it is an exploration of the concept of 'knowing'.

Life, Death and Renewal

(Selected Poems 2008-1988)

Fire for Easter

Phoenix
Lost in peace
Still moments
Of serene
Aether
Fuelled
To ascend
Cast off ashes
Burn eagerly
Calmly
Against this
Cold world
Its cold people

Shifting coals
Woods
Yielding
To the flame
Now shooting up
Intense in purpose
Heat
Calorific
Taking with it
Aeons
Of deposits
Carbon data
Solidified souls
Vegetation
For the ashes

Joanne Maria McNally

To return to clay
Awaiting
Some renewal

Stories, lies
Shrivelled
To a cinder
Reduced to an atom
A single ember

Flames furling
Coals
Curling logs
Tinder, wood
Quickening
Combustion:
Will the coal run out
Will the wood run out
And the oil
Before redemption?

Fire
Oblivious
To burning lies
Or truth
It burns
And renews
Burns and renews
Millennia
Prometheus's gift to us
We've used

And abused
Burnt people alive
Annihilated
Forests
Primeval refuge

Flames piercing
To the heart
Layers
Peel apart
Lives tear asunder
Histories crumble
Coals darken
Glows ashen
With the rhythm
Sound
Irregular
Of centuries passing

Furious crackling
Then spatting
Finally
Subsides
To a lulling melody
Of flickering notes
Of
Divine fire
Saving
Sparks
Of lost souls

Igniting gently
The pulse
To self-renewal

Brondesbury Rd, London, March 2008

Images after the Black Rain
(For War-torn Civilians)

We meet you on a journey
From terror and war to exile
From the Black Rain
We approach you
Draw close
Curious about the images:
This is you
This is your life, you say
And your death
We see the tomb.
Yet it is much more.

We can't follow you.
There's no linearity,
No composition.
There's no centre.
Or so it seems

Viewpoints shift
Perspectives sink
Into self-sufficient
Diversity
Chaotic diversity?
Incoherence, perhaps.
Singles, couples
Loners, faces
Animals, trees

Fish
Nature
Rise from the wash
Equally
Interconnecting
Easily
Yet remain estranged.
This is no new Eden.

There is dynamism
Yet containment
Not restlessness
Universal movement
Moments
But no real direction
And it doesn't matter
It seems

The present is detailed
Incredibly peopled
Crowded
The future unseen

Or rather under tension
As we're pulled
In opposing directions

We step back
Draw back
And only then
Perceive

The unresolved dilemma
The moment on the cross
The kneeling figure

A unity emerges
Unintended?
A plane hovers
Not with bombs:
It offers flight

Brondesbury Rd, London, March 2008

Freedom of Mind in Rosa
(In memory of Rosa Luxemburg, 1871-1919)

Still I am a corpse
Quite unconscious
Wild was the storm
More wild
Than I'd imagined
Then
When my work
Was all
My people
All

Now I float to the surface
Quite slowly
Almost silently
In the wake of atrocities
Atrocities
Also in my wake –
I couldn't prevent them.
Now I'm moved
To and fro
Still trapped in the basin
As in a witch's cauldron
Knocked from all sides

How long still
How long before I'll be

Before I'll really be?

Thrown away
Like putrid meat
After being beaten
Shot
Fleeced
In the depth of winter.
Now I float
Veiled in darkness
Alone
In ice-cold water
Far from the chaos
Bloodbath
And hunt:
Songs of ill will
Dissipated
Hate campaigns
Dispelled
Murderous chants
Dispersed

With head intact
I float and reflect:

No more I'll lead
That's passed
Now I am
And will yet be.
Differently
I think

About people
Animals, justice
The world.
My work?
It's not yet done
As I'd wished –
Its dawn awaits

The compass points
To new directions
I am awakened
I rise to the sun
Stride forth
Turn my head
Look behind
And see –
Many follow:
They are the free

Grimsby, July 2007 (translated from German
version, composed in Berlin, January 2004)

Edina

Edina, Scotia's darling seat!
Hailed Burns in staunchly reverence
To claim, and claim, and claim again
Old Scotland's rightful existence
Through idiom in verse and song
A nation born of hallowed tongue

Edina, braw bairn no more bow!
Formed of twin volcanic brow
With rugged seat and belly fired
Solidified, then edified
With castle crown
With nature's fertile gown

Edina, Muse on stately dome
Friend to strangers, to bards a home
Formed of curving seams and nodules
Stratified with values social
Crowned with crags of steadfast lives
With writers lost whose fame survives

Edina, willows stroke your feet
Whisper glories, defy defeat
Clothe the deep gorge of old Nor' Loch
Border scarred times of Castle Rock
Still visible 'neath works of men
And coverings of peaks and glen

Edina, buoyed by Arthur's strength
Commanding awe and natural sense
Scanning waters of the North
Surveying isles amidst the Forth
Girded by mighty span of steel
Enriched by strands of commonweal

Edina, with sovereign power reclaimed
Fairness, good faith impart your name
Embrace a multitude of views
Imbue your bairns with love of truth
Edina, arise from your bowed state
Dawn beckons your righteousness, your grace!

Edinburgh, July 2007

* This poem is an echo back to Robert Burns' poem 'Address to Edinburgh', and pays tribute to contemporary Edinburgh and Scotland and to my own Scottish roots (Wemyss clan).
I use the term 'commonweal' for common welfare, public good.

Mother Womb

At birth
We cry
That we've come
To this great
Stage of fools
Leaving suspense
Water
And nurture
Of a womb
To be cast
Into a pool
Of unending strife
Folly, Furies
Eventual doom
Yet striving for
Encountering
At times rekindling
Glories of the womb:
Vibrant peace
Pulsing serenity
Oneness of being
Beating not time
Nor deadlines
But of hearts
Sensually attuned
Creating zest
Desire
Wellness of being

Sealing dust
- celestial dust
With love
Water, genes
Generating life
Anew
And perpetual
Within
And from
An all embracing
Universal
Mother Womb

Grimsby, 18 March 2007

* I see this poem as a celebration of my mother, of life and of life's possibilities, in spite of the stage of fools who often govern us and lead us into massive tragedies and suffering. Our Universe and Earth are beautiful and renewing, and for me, the Universe is like a mother womb.

Love's Creation

A whirlwind
Stroked my heart:

Quietly
Seductively
Hot circling air
Caressed
My swelling breast
Pitched
The voice within
Then receded
To the night
Whisking
Its dark secret

To return
Revived in strength
Passion
And insistence
Orbiting yet more
Closely
Penetrating
More deeply
Creating waves
To move me
Onwards
Onwards
Wanting more

Till we begin
To flow
Ever freely
Sensuously
Within
This circling life
Our spirits
Stirred as one:
Fiery air
Earthy water
Into a primeval
Force –

A vortex
Of Creation

Grimsby, September 2006

Black and White Sisters

Here they come
Up the street
One in quick time
Tiny hurried feet
The other slow
Graceful
Swinging her hips,
One is wary
Attentive and sharp
The other serene
Gregarious
Not quick to bark,
One loves food
In all shapes
And sizes
The other holds back
Preferring
Hot spices,
One tosses a ball
In mad circles
Round the room
The other watches
At a distance
Totally unmoved,
One snuggles up close
In need of affection
The other looks on
Waiting for her moment,

Then at night
In the quiet
When darkness descends
They lie down together
Almost as one

Weelsby Rd, Grimsby, August 2006

Between the Devil and The Deep
(*Song in Harmony for New Orleans*)

The Devil from beneath
The mighty deep
And the sea rolls on
And on rolls the sea
Concealed in a chasm
Way out of sight
Once disturbed
Called forth
Will fright
On and on
Rolls the sea
Spew forth
Its venom
Its venom from beneath
The blue azure
Of the shimmering sea
Rolls on
And on and on
Rolls the sea

Gorging, deforming
All in its wake
And on
And on
Rolls the sea
Engulfing
Plundering
Those in its way
And on

And on
Rolls the sea
Rendering all asunder
Confounding their say
And the heart
Of the sea
Beats
On and on

Pulling families apart
Putting folks at war
And on and on
Rolls the sea
Turning friend
Against friend
And the heart
Of the sea
Beats on and on

And its tongue extends
Spreading slime
Through a fork
And on
And on
Rolls the sea
Smearing drudge
And dirt
Till it sticks
And heaves
And on
And on
Rolls the sea

And the heart
Of the sea
Our heart – you see
Rolls on
And on
Harbours spirits
Of calm
And calls
From the deep
Rolls on and on
And way out
In the deep
The devil
Still lurks
And on
And on
Roll the peril
And wonders
Of the deep blue sea

Grimsby, 28 Aug 2005

Let it be!

No!
Don't do it
I thought
Yet couldn't
Quite say,
Don't hit
That poor thing
Don't pursue
That prey

It's a right
To exist
It belongs here
Like you
It wants
Just to live
It loves
To be free

What right
Have you
Got
To aim there
To kill?
No right
I should shout
Yet still
Cannot say

Why can't I
I think
Why can't I
Say?
Why can't I
Shout
For its rights
Shout for it
To be

I'm no better
Than them
That aim
There to kill
I sit here
And stare
I should
Stand up
And shout
Shout out
And not
Fear
Shout out
LET IT BE!

Hove, 27 July 2005

* *On the killing of a seagull (youngsters throwing stones at it on the beach) at about the same time as the assassination of the Brazilian Jean Charles de Menezes in the London Underground.*

She-Line

See your grandma
In your mother
See her face
Fold into hers
Feel time
Concertina
Lost memories
Seep forth
Sense yourself
In your niece
Now there
Where
You were once
Life stretching
Out before her
Spring, summer
And fall
As winter
Creeps
Upon your mother
While mid summer
Keeps you tall

Grimsby, August 2004

The Presence

'May I join you?'
Asked the figure
So softly
And politely
From the side
Of the bed,
'Are you ready
To embrace me
To let me lull you
And lead you
To the sleep
Of all sleeps?'

Its slender fair hand
Tugged tenderly
At the sheet,
And sliding towards me
Very slowly
I perceived
Its lace-woven sleeve
And fine cloth
Of its attire
Fluttering faintly
With the breeze

In awe of the presence
I knew not quite
What to say
But observed

Almost calmly
As it lifted the sheet
Most lithely
And started
To approach me
Tacitly
In its own way

Succumbing
To the moment
To the strangeness
Of its touch,
I could feel
My heart expanding
Opening
Rising
To welcome it
As such:
I wanted to embrace it
For it to join me in sleep
And my mind drifted
Languorously
Pleasurably
Towards the promise
Of its peace

As the presence drew nearer
And its figure increased
Wistly
Seductively
It beheld me

In a stillness
In a quietness
Quite different
From sleep –
I was stirred
By a silence
So serene
So complete
I was lulled to the rhythm
Of its dance at my feet

I could feel
My wan limbs weaken,
To the soulfulness
Of its beat,
And then float
Towards the motion
Mellow with its heat,
Then mould into its dance –
Its dance
Of flickering flame –
Almost within reach

And as its garment of lace
Merged into a blinding
Shaft of light
I sensed my body rise
And move towards
A mystery
Stranger than life

Joanne Maria McNally

I drifted along
Without weight
Time or stress,
A swathe
Of ethereal light
My only form of dress –

When all of a sudden
On the verge of white light
A blackbird
Burst into song
And broke through the night,
It welcomed the morn
The dawn
Of a new day,
It sang out its heart
In its own way

'I'm not ready!'
I contested,
Though the presence
Was no longer felt,
'I've work still to do
I've things still to say
I've songs still to sing
In my own way –
I know you'll be back
It's a matter
Only of time

But till that day,
When your flame
Comes
To extinguish mine,
I'll burn with a brightness
I'll dance against time.'

Berlin, April 2004

One Day

One-day
Fly
Dancing
Life's song
Dancing
On air-
Streams
Westerly
Easterly
Dancing
Free

And we?

Must we
Live
Yet longer
To be
Less free
More
Dispensed
Administered
Fettered
By files
Woven
Into websites
Freez'd
Till we dance
No more

No longer
See

We need
Not pity
A one-day
Fly
It tastes
More Life
Than we
In our
Shackled
Blinkered
Longevity

Hove, September 2004

Germany in November

Figures like Lowry's
Stooped in grey
Shrouded in the mist
And dullness
Of a day
Without a beginning
Cross Alexanderplatz
On their way
To work
To shop
Dwarfed
By concrete monstrosities
Bent by Siberian winds

As we roll
Southwards
On plastic-cushioned seats
Lit by lamps
Shaped like tears

Wind generators
Poplar trees
Embroider
Flat landscapes
Blobs of red
Yellow, green leaves
In between
Ghost-factories
Chimneys long dead

Life, Death and Renewal

Competing
With wind-swept
Trunks
Of spindly fir-trees

As we speed
Southwards
On plastic-cushioned seats
Consuming
Bread rolls and tea

Scars of mined wounds
Pockmark the flatness
Gape
Into the greyness
Of a day
Broken
By mounds
Flattened on top
Made-over
To conceal
Gorged-out caverns
Beneath

As we race
Southwards
On plastic-cushioned seats
With a view
Shaped like tears

Brigades
Of wind generators
Swing their arms

Joanne Maria McNally

In time
To currents of air
Neat strips of trees
Line
Green-carpeted heaps
While small farmsteads
And dull-yellow houses
Huddle round
Rare churches
Almost unseen

As we rush
Through the East
On plastic-cushioned seats
With our light
Shaped like tears

Forty shades of amber
Thrust
Out of Undulating
Thuringian
Scarps of pink
Black chequered houses
Nestle in slopes
Laced
By willow-swept streams
Interlocked
By greyish-white
Outcrops
And bunched-up pines

Life, Death and Renewal

As we weave
Southwards
On plastic-cushioned seats
Warmed by lamps
Shaped like tears

Snakelike contours
Reed-threaded brooks
Glimpses of sunlight
Now in between
On a mill-pond
Six geese swim:
White geese
Beneath
A Bavarian blue sky
As fields of goats
And churches increase
Unscathed
By bloody battles
And harsh industry

As we race
Southwards
Then westwards
Without light
Shaped like tears

Squeaky clean cars
No Trabi in sight
Freshly washed
Windows
Refracting
Sunlight

Joanne Maria McNally

Colours and forms
Encampments of hens
Lining tracks
Caravans and tents
Crowding
Lakes well-kempt:
Even the gravel pits reflect
A clearly groomed style

As we rush
To nowhere
On plastic-cushioned seats
With light
Made of tears

Berlin, November 2003

Drowned by a Tear

Clasping you tenderly
In my hands
Before you faded
Completely
I saw the aphid
In your heart
Siphoning your last juices,
Before you perished
Entirely
And in an act of defiance
A tear from my eye
Drowned the parasite
Within

Berlin, November 2003

* *At a local level this is a poem about illness taking hold of a beloved person and the helplessness that the friend, lover, member of the family feels as they see the person being ravaged by it.*
At a global level it's the illness /destructive seed and the destructive forces at the heart of a beloved country or continent such as Africa.

Eternity

In pain
Before death
We had only minutes;
You didn't know
Death's pull
Was so close –

Or did you?

You heard me speak
I think you heard –
Our oneness felt
So complete

I heard no sounds –
Your eyes expressed
What I couldn't grasp
Only sense

I spoke intensely
Reassuringly
Stroking you
Affirming
My love

I spoke the same words
Again and again
Like a chant
Praying they'd reach you

As you slipped
To where
You were heading
Away from my side

Holding on to your eyes
With mine
You became distant
They became darker –
Filled
With a never-ending
Depth

I was looking into Eternity

Hove, 12 November 2003

Red wine with Snowdrops

Our anger declined
As down your temples
Over fear-worn skin
Trickles of wine
Slowly weaved
Jerkily
Through creases
Passed your skin
To your vest –
Arrested
By the cloth
White-bleached

Stunned
Silenced
By this 'act of violence'
In a moment of heat
This response
To drunken words
And actions
Unplanned
Yet so sweet –
Born out of passion
A glass of red wine
Anointing your head
Was the best
Means I could find

Ps)

As dawn
Did its stirring
I returned to the scene:
Gone
Were the stain
Glass and red wine.
Did it happen
The anointment?
Your vest looked as clean
As the snowdrops
On the table
Still there
Where you had been

Hove, August 2003

* This image, first created in this short poem, plays a key role in the turning point of 'Hell Unlimited. Where Shakespeare met Goethe' (2008)

Gypsy Thoughts

Dressed up in clothes
Fit for the city
Lily-white skin
Hair knotted back
Sophisticated
Sleek
You wander
Meander
Away from,
Beyond
And back to your roots

You travel the mind
Free and resilient
Stopping
Diverting
Lingering on paths
Stubborn
Strong
Wild and defiant
You let them expand
Connect and contract

Pulled on by nature
Energy and loving
Unfettered rhythms
Betray where you're from –

Joanne Maria McNally

Exotic
Nomadic
Your course is a dance
Lining your skin
Inflecting your song

Hove, August 2003

* *For individuals leading unconventional lives and following their true nature.*

Grim's Lament

'Boarded up shops
Still open but closed
To natural light
And street vandals outside.
Is this really my town?'
Asked Odin through Grim
To which Havelock replied –

'You've been starved of all funds
You've paid over the odds
The country you're part of
Threw you back to the Gods,
The Pope didn't want you
Excommunicat'd your lot
False charges were brought,
They left you to rot.

Yet, the Great in your name
Is not there by mistake
Not through bribes or smooth-talking
It's there for Great's sake,
It's deep in your soul
Despite the soft ground
The sand may be shifting
But your town remains sound.
You've blessed ancient mariners
Who harvest far-flung shores
You've guarded the heroes

Fallen warriors of yore,
With your eight-legged horse
And disguises so plenty
You've wandered the world
Reversing all enmity.

But now you're back with us
Your work can proceed
We'll start with the fishermen
Their families are in need.'

Grim pulled his cloak tighter
Secured his brimmed hat
And with a wink and a nod
Duly follow'd Havelock.

Abbotsway, Grimsby, May 2003

* *According to tradition, Great Grimsby was founded by Havelock the Dane, and his life was saved by a Grimsby fisherman called Grim. Grim(r) is one of Odin's many disguises. 'Grima' is the word for a large hood.*
According to legend, the town was excommunicated due to an incident involving a monk at the abbey in Grimsby, in which the townsfolk were falsely blamed.

Grand Old Dame!

(*The Collapse of the West Pier, Brighton*)

You stand by the New
Misshapen by elements
Ravaged by time,
Sunken in the middle
With your bow still held high

You ponder the New -
At its head
Gay amusements
Noisy chaos within,
No sags in the middle
Taut props for *its* bed -
At *your* feet The Grand

Your sudden collapse
In the storm, caused alarm
Spurred into action
Photographers, dignitaries, townsfolk
To capture, inspect you
Toast your honour,
What treatment
Will they lavish on
You?
Will they patch you, botox you
Rebuild you as new?
Have they asked you
If you want to start anew?

Or will they let nature
Work you
Mould you as hers,
Until she has you
Complete
And dispersed
In the world?

Yet rumours abound
They'll blast you away -
Alas, Grand Old Dame!
Acts of violence
May still end,
Your natural decay

Hove, 6 January 2003

* The Grand is also the name of the hotel which was bombed in 1979. The Pier was also damaged by arsonist attacks.

Westbury Station at Christmas

Cold winds blow through
Plastic flowers swing
Beneath the steely sky
Streaked with hues of blue
Dappled with blobs of sun

Between a make-shift kiosk
And a diet coke machine
A small Christmas tree
Stands propped -
An oversize bucket
Its dwelling,
Dazzling shades of tinsel
Slung round its waist, in haste
Distract the eye's attention
Blur its natural shape

The Quantocks, December 2002

Silesia in December

Shrouded in mist

Fields of waterlogged

Sand

Dark-coloured peat,

Stunted fir-trees

Beneath

Skeletal pines

Long black trunks

Silver

Inbetween

Silesia, December 2002

Beyond

Watching the Sea

Beyond myself

Feeling

Waves erode

Mountains

Sun evaporate

Clouds

Within

Hove, November 2002

Crossroads of Hell

Marching not knowing
Why or whither

In winter
Twenty below zero
Over mountains

Weeks and miles
On end

Without coats, boots
Food –

In a bad way we were
Till we saw the others

Without shirts, shoes
Souls

Empty of spirit
Painfully thin

The last breath of being
Whipped out of them

Why, what for?

Marching without knowing

Berlin, February 2002

Synthesis

Together
Searching dawn
Cold steps
Warm talk
Hand on chest
Sudden spark –
Toe on toes
Tears on lashes
Tongue on toes
Lips on lashes,
Playing in water
Entwined in the dark
Stroking fingers
Double rainbow
Silent mist
Fingers on muscles –
Kneading
Caressing
Stroking
By a stream
– moonlit
Looking out to sea
Synthesised

Brighton, May 1991

Separating

Solitary shadows

Displaced

Feel their way

Through lonely streets

Stroking each other

Only rarely

In tentative rhythms

Of departure

Exeter, June 1990

Duck's Mood

She swims and circles

Without a goal

Floats

Against the stream

Pleased

Unaware of her exhaustion

She laughs with her tail

When the mainland's

Reached

Berlin, Germany, February 1988

Plant and Water

Flowing with the stream

Swaying to the motion

Of endless time

Endless water

You sweep the seabed

Rising and falling

To the perpetuating

Pulsating

Rhythm of life

Konstanz, Germany, 19 January 1988
(for my father)

Some Personal Reflections on Poetry And on 'XChanges'

It is thanks to a wonderful treasure of illustrated poetry selected, and commented on by Louis Untermeyer, and which my parents gave me at the age of five, that my love for poetry was sealed. And some of my earliest recollections are of sitting by an open fire at my grandmother's house in Binbrook, Lincolnshire, blissfully reading from this book (which, incidentally, I still have and keep by my bedside), absorbing what I was reading, though probably understanding very little at that time.

Poetry, at its best, has the power, nevertheless, to get under the skin – and sometimes in an instant. And, it can surface as a primeval 'sign', a voice, a vision, a feeling or a thought. Perhaps poetry is the only form of deep truth.

At its most subliminal, poetry can respond to and capture the essence of a being, a thing, a moment, a place, a situation, an idea or a feeling, and it can also transcend these. The ultimate creative ambition of poetry is still perhaps to become a 'Redeemer of the human mind' (Ralph Waldo Emerson, 1840); the physician which humanity desperately needs now more than ever.
And, poetry can also be a kind of wake-up call across time and space; that is to say, a Redeemer of the human race. This is perhaps best achieved when there is the sense of a living being behind the poetry – a full-bloodied person with attitude, vision and perspective: think of Shelley; think of Adrienne Rich.

'XChanges' was the name I gave to poems which I wrote in notebooks over six years ago. It seems appropriate to keep the name: 'XChanges' is organic and has expanded, contracted and evolved over time in response to inner and outer impulses; that is to say, exchanges and transformations. The majority of the poems in this collection have evolved since 2002 – the year when I began to concentrate most intensely on creative writing, and in particular on poetry, as this is where my heart, body and mind seem most at one when I write. I believe this is reflected in the style which is largely free-flowing with internal rhythms and internal rhymes or half-rhymes. Usually I do not impose a form on the content – I let the first line, initial idea or image speak to me in its own tone, pitch, pattern and rhythm. Such poems include 'Bones of War', 'The Presence', and also 'Knowing'. 'Knowing' is a spontaneous impulse to what Hugh MacDiarmid called 'difficult knowledge', and was written on one day, although I had been researching and thinking about this particular 'difficult knowledge' for some months before the form impulsively emerged. For me, 'Gypsy Thoughts' captures this process of allowing thoughts and feelings to meander, collide, coincide and separate.

Poems where the form is more deliberate include 'An Autumn Suffering', 'Rosa in Montefiorino', 'Edina' and 'Grim's Lament'. 'Grim's Lament' is also the inspiration for my epic poem 'Odin's Best Horse' (2006, not yet in print) which follows a traditional form of four line stanzas with end-rhyme, while addressing the contemporary world's disorders.

Free-flowing also means that I tend to avoid too much punctuation – preferring instead a certain layout and patterning on the page, and a certain open-endedness (that is to say, open-mindedness) both in form and meaning. Indeed, I do not avoid ambiguity – I try and embrace the full weight and meaning of words by allowing for layers and fluidity: often words and lines can simultaneously be connected to the previous line or word and to the following one, especially with the absence of punctuation. For me, this reflects life: meaningful, flowing and multi-layered; life which is not empty, overly constrained or functionally-orientated, and which is toing and froing, and is forward-looking and backward-glancing. However, whenever I have deemed it necessary, I have indicated in the notes my own impulse or association behind the poem.

And free-flowing means breaking the tyranny and censorship not only of established views but of the conscious, and letting words and images have free play, and 'creatively misbehave' at will.

And as the whole of the mind should be wide open and 'ought to have a mother as well as a father!' (Virginia Woolf)), I have included the poem 'Mother Womb' which alludes to the Universe – the Mother of all Creation – as being like a 'Mother Womb'.

And, on this note, I would like to pay special thanks, not only to my own mother and father in encouraging me to write, and keep writing poetry, but also to Tessa Ransford (Edinburgh) and Jenni Calder (Edinburgh), Saadi Yousef (London) and Elazar Benyoetz (Jerusalem). I am greatly indebted to their support and encouragement. 'An Italian Collection' is also a response to Saadi Yousef's suggestion that I could 'put more flesh on the bones'.

Special thanks also to Claudio Pozzani (poet and initiator and organiser of the new poetry festival 'European Voices', 2008) for inviting me to present some of my poems in Berlin, along with their translations in German, at the dawn of this exciting literary development.

Contents